VOLUME THREE

TRAINS in TROUBLE

RAILWAY ACCIDENTS IN PICTURES

Ken Hoole

THE AUTHOR

Ken Hoole has for many years specialised in the history of the North Eastern Railway, and all that entails, but he has had a long interest in railway accidents in Great Britain, no matter which company was involved. As a schoolboy he collected files of newspaper cuttings dealing with railway accidents, starting with the Hull accident of 1927 and the Darlington collision of 1928, and has continued collecting to the present day.

Ken Hoole has written 27 books and co-operated in many others, all on railways and associated subjects, and has others in the pipeline. He has agreed to compile Volume 4 in the *Trains in Trouble* series.

THE PHOTOGRAPHS

Unless otherwise indicated, all the photographs in this book are from the author's own collection.

First published 1982   © K. Hoole 1982

ISBN 0 906899 05 2

Designed by Nigel Trevena

Printed by Century Litho. Tel: Falmouth 311747

Published by
**ATLANTIC
TRANSPORT & HISTORICAL
PUBLISHERS**
25 Scorrier Street St Day Redruth
Cornwall TR16 5LH
Telephone (0209) 821016

Introduction

What is the fascination of railway accidents that has made the *Trains in Trouble* series such a success? Accidents bring tragedy to the passengers and staff involved, but the effects can be much more far reaching.

Railway accidents have always been newsworthy; witness the pages of newspaper coverage of any major collision or derailment, and now there is television coverage. Enterprising publishers of picture postcards have often cashed in by producing sets of cards of notable accidents, and numerous books have been written on the subject.

But why are so many railway enthusiasts interested? I prefer to think that it is not because of any morbid interest, but rather to see what went wrong with our railway system where the safety of the passenger has been or paramount importance since the early days of carriage by rail, with speeds unheard of in horse-and-cart days.

The most interesting reading on the subject is undoubtedly found in the Board of Trade Reports, which are still published by the Stationery Office for the Department of Transport. These Reports show the weakness and strength, not only of the materials and equipment, but also of the passengers and staff caught up in a situation not of their own choosing.

Human nature, being what it is, has been responsible for many accidents brought about by forgetfulness, over confidence, negligence, or even spite. Trains have, at times, been deliberately derailed because of some real or imagined grievance, but fortunately occurrences of this sort have been in the minority.

My interest in railway accidents goes back more than fifty years, and in that time I have collected newspaper accounts of every major British accident, and many minor ones, and although press reports are not always accurate they do, when read in conjunction with the Board of Trade Report, provide background information not always brought out at the official enquiry.

I have read virtually every Report published over the last century, and Reports concerning the North Eastern Railway almost since its inception in 1854. Time and time again it is stressed that the formal Enquiry is being held primarily to discover why and how the accident happened, so that steps could be taken to ensure that a similar accident could not occur again. On occasions, when a Report has named the person considered to be responsible for the accident, a charge of manslaughter has been brought against a driver or signal-man. A fairly recent example was Driver Frew who was involved in the December 1957 St Johns disaster, when 88 passengers were killed. He was twice tried for manslaughter but acquitted.

At one time it was the practice to fine railway staff for minor infringements of the Rules; more serious offences could lead to some days suspension without pay; or demotion from express driver to shunting engine driver. In some cases a driver was dismissed, bringing disgrace to the man and hardship to his family. Even drivers involved in accidents caused by the faults of others felt the effects so deeply that they were unable to drive again. Even though they may not have been physically injured the worry could bring an early death.

Thus the study of accidents can bring a deep insight into human behaviour, as well as the reason for a signal not functioning correctly, or why a piece of equipment on a locomotive broke for no apparent reason. All these details add to our knowledge of railways past and present. *K. HOOLE*

FURTHER VOLUMES
Volumes 1 and 2 in the *Trains in Trouble* series were compiled by the late Arthur Trevena and included the best of his remarkable collection of British railway accident photographs. They are both available from booksellers or, plus 35p p&p, from the publishers.

Volume 4, compiled by Ken Hoole, will comprise an authoritative examination of a variety of different types of accident, grouped according to their cause, and copiously illustrated with photographs which will be quite unknown to the general reader. The book's publication, during 1983, will be announced in the railway press, but readers requiring personal notification are invited to send an s.a.e. to the publishers.

OPPOSITE: The 8.00 am Tunbridge Wells to Brighton train derailed at Crowborough; 3rd April 1916. (Full details elsewhere). *Photo: Collection the late Arthur Trevena*
RIGHT: The aftermath of the Abermule disaster, 26th January 1921. (Full details elsewhere).
TITLE PAGE: 0-6-0 No.1245 being rerailed after the accident at Lingdale Junction; 5th November 1900. (Full details elsewhere).

THE BRIDGE IS DOWN

Poor workmanship, lax supervision, and the failure to appreciate the effects of extreme wind pressure on large structures, contributed to the collapse of the Tay Bridge on the exceptionally stormy evening of Sunday 28th December 1879 just as the 5.20 pm train from Burntisland to Dundee (with passengers from Edinburgh) was passing over it.

Much of the ironwork was cast by the Middlesbrough firm of Hopkins, Gilkes & Co., which also built locomotives and had close connections with railways in north eastern England. At the subsequent Board of Trade enquiry it was disclosed that much shoddy work and material had gone into the bridge, which had been opened in the previous year. The designer of the bridge was Thomas Bouch, who had been knighted for his work on it.

It was estimated that there were 69 passengers and six railwaymen (and probably some small children) travelling on the train and all were drowned when the engine and all the coaches plunged into the Tay.

Old Tay Bridge Disaster. The Ten

TOP RIGHT: The engine, 4-4-0 No.224, after being lifted from the bed of the River Tay.
BOTTOM RIGHT: The tender from No.224.

ABOVE: When the fallen girders from the ill-fated Tay Bridge were eventually recovered it was found that they had fallen on the east side of the structure and had settled on the river bed on their eastern face, still with some of the coaches inside the framework of metal. In this view the girders are standing on their side, with the base of the bridge, complete with single track, standing vertically on the right.

Photo: Collection the late Arthur Trevena

The Tay Bridge disaster (continued)

NEARER RIGHT: The watch (by Thos.
Russell & Son of Liverpool) carried by
the guard of the train.
FAR RIGHT: Tickets collected at St Fort
before the train reached the Tay Bridge.

BELOW: The remains of the Tay Bridge,
with some of the fallen girders in the
river.

This Watch was found on the Guard
of the Passenger Train that fell with
the Tay Bridge Disaster, 28th Dec.,
1879.

These Tickets were Collected at St Fort Station, on 28th December, 1879, by Robert Morris, Agent;
Wm. Friend, Ticket Collector; and Alex. Inglis, Porter, from the Passengers
who lost their lives by the Fall of the Tay Bridge.

FALLEN ROCK BLOCKS GOODS

On 16th February 1880, the 1.00 pm goods from Monmouth to Chepstow ran into a large rock that had fallen from the hillside on the east side of the railway, 1½ miles south of Chepstow. The rock was part of the foundations of a retaining wall which carried the Coleford Tramway, built some sixty years previously on a formation higher up the hillside than the later Monmouth-Chepstow line.

When the engine hit the rock (which had not been seen by the driver and fireman) it was derailed and overturned, coming to rest wheels uppermost. The driver was pinned underneath, although he was safely extricated by a breaksman *(sic)* who was travelling in the van with the guard.

The engine was built at Wolverhampton in 1870 and not withdrawn until 1930.

Photo: L&GRP Collection, courtesy David & Charles

NIGHT COLLISION IN KENT

In the early hours of 7th June 1884 the 6.00 pm goods from Deal to London ran into the rear of the 10.00 pm goods from Folkestone to London in Sevenoaks station. The Folkestone goods was about to stop to take water when the Deal train, which was not booked to stop, crashed into it at about 25 mph. The train from Deal consisted of two engines and 38 loaded wagons, with a brake van front and rear; the leading engine (0-6-0 No.1) was badly damaged and the driver and fireman were killed, but the crew on the train engine (0-6-0 No.294) were unhurt when their engine fell over on to its left side. Engine No.1 was built in 1868 and it was reboilered following this collision, only to be withdrawn in 1890; No.294 was built in 1879 and withdrawn in 1909. This view shows No.294 on its side.

The accident was caused by confusion between two signalmen, with the man at Sevenoaks not restoring his signals immediately so that both trains were running under the same clear signals.

Photo: Collection the late Arthur Trevena

GATESHEAD 1890

TROUBLE ON THE INCLINE

Little is known of this mishap which took place in 1890 on Redheugh Incline, Gateshead. The incline was originally rope worked, with a steam hauling engine near Gateshead West station, but changed to locomotive working as engines improved, and it appears as if the engine was derailed as it was descending the incline running bunker first, with its train piling up around it. The engine was NER No.811 of Class E, perhaps better known as LNER Class J71, then only three years old. It continued to run until 1937.

MATERIAL PROBLEMS

On 1st May 1891 the 8.45 am from Brighton to London was derailed as it was crossing a cast iron bridge spanning Portland Road at Norwood Junction. The engine was 0-4-2 No.175 *Hayling* and it was brought to a stop with the last vehicle of the 12-coach train actually standing on the defective bridge. Later in the day, as clearing-up operations were taking place, the damaged girder gave way completely, allowing the rear van to fall vertically into the roadway below, with one end on the ground and the other projecting slightly above track level *(circled in the lower picture).*

The suitability of cast iron bridges had been in doubt for some time and this accident led to a nationwide investigation into, and the renewal of, cast iron structures.

*Photos: (top) R.C. Riley collection
(bottom) Collection the late Arthur Trevena*

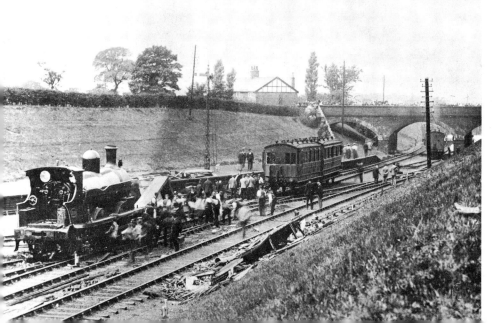

EXCURSION TRAIN IN TROUBLE

At 6.05 am on the morning of 3rd August a 14-coach load of happy passengers left Leeds for Blackpool behind Lancashire & Yorkshire 0-6-0 No.1058. At Preston Junction, 2 miles south of Preston station, the excursion train was stopped at a ticket platform on a loop off the main line for tickets to be collected, and for the engine to take water. When ready to leave the signal for the excursion standing in the loop remained at danger and the signalman cleared the main line signals for a West Lancashire train bound for Preston. However, the driver of the Blackpool train took the signal as his own and, after a whistle, he moved off — just as the West Lancashire train was passing. The resulting sidelong collision damaged three coaches of the West Lancashire train, killing one passenger and injuring 7 others. The L&Y engine was damaged but its train was unscathed.

Photo: Collection the late Arthur Trevena

TOO FAST IN WALES

This derailment, which occurred on 11th June 1897, involved another excursion train, this time with two engines, and the Inspecting Officer concluded that it was due to poor track and excessive speed. A feature of this accident was the severe damage sustained by the coaches of mixed Cambrian and Lancashire & Yorkshire origin: the bodies were completely wrecked and 11 passengers killed. The engines were Cambrian 0-6-0s Nos.75 and 77 (later GWR Nos.878 and 880), both built by Neilson & Co. in 1894.

Photos: Collection the late Arthur Trevena

LINGDALE JUNCTION 1900

RECOVERING No.1245

The accident at Lingdale Junction on 5th November 1900 took place at the junction of two mineral branches near Brotton, then in the North Riding of Yorkshire; both branches are now closed and lifted. A train-load of ironstone descending from Lingdale Mines got out of control on the 1 in 36 gradient and was derailed at trap points at the junction with the Kilton branch. The engine was 0-6-0 No.1245, built at Darlington in 1873, which was running tender first. At this point the line was on an embankment and when No.1245 was derailed it fell on to its right-hand side on the slope of the embankment. It was recovered using two sets of block and tackle anchored to the rails, on which an engine stood to keep them in place. Two further engines were attached to the tackle and as they moved away from one another No.1245 was pulled upright, and held until two steam cranes could get hold to rerail it.

See also page 1

Photo: Collection the late Arthur Trevena

INTO THE POND

On 27th June 1905, McDonnell 0-6-0 No.1486 was working a goods train towards Newcastle, running tender first, when it was derailed at Church Pit Crossing signalbox, Wallsend, on the line from Tynemouth. At this point the Seaton Burn wagonway was crossed on the level by the North Eastern line and it appears that the engine and tender were derailed on the crossing and then ran down the bank into a pond!

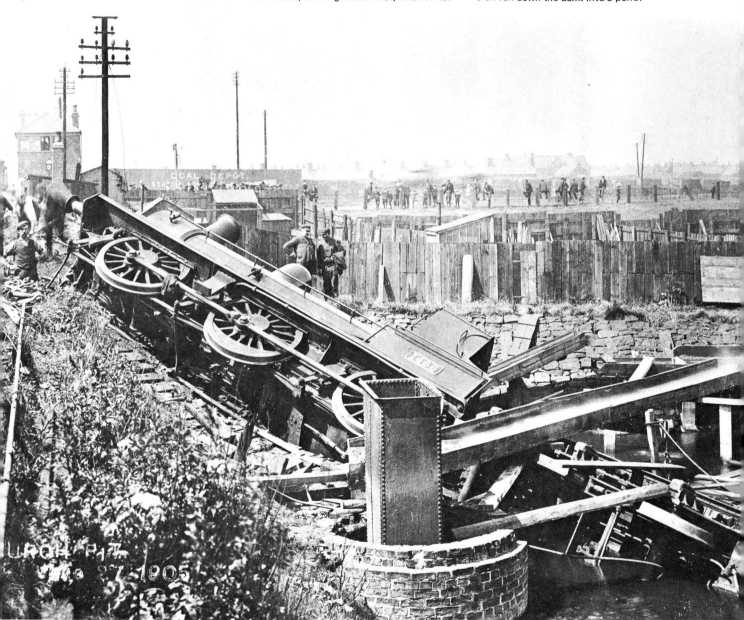

DRAMA OF THE NIGHT EXPRESS

The reason for his high speed derailment was never discovered. The train involved was the 8.45 pm from Kings Cross to Edinburgh on 19th September 1906, which failed to make a scheduled stop in Grantham station. Instead, it ran through the station at speed, passing at danger the signals at the north end of the platform. The train was derailed on the reverse curves leading to the Nottingham branch, for which the points were set at the time because an up goods from the branch to the main line had just passed.

The engine, Ivatt Atlantic No.276, which had taken over the train at Peterborough, fell on to its left-hand side and remained in line with the down branch on an embankment, but the tender and the leading five coaches were deflected into a yard at the foot of the embankment. Unfortunately the driver and fireman were killed, together with nine passengers and a Post Office mail van attendant; two other passengers subsequently died from their injuries.

This was the second of three similar accidents, the others being at Salisbury earlier in 1906 and at Shrewsbury in 1907.

The picture shows the severe damage to the footplate of the Atlantic.

NO CERTAIN CAUSE

In the lesser-known rear-end collision at Ulleskelf (on the York to Normanton/Leeds line) again the crew was killed and no certain cause of the accident was discovered, although it was suggested that the driver may have been concentrating on 'racing' a Lancashire & Yorkshire train on an adjacent track. The North Eastern engine — Class F1 4-4-0 No.85 — was in the hands of a Hull crew working Hull-Scarborough-York-Leeds-Hull, a triangular duty of a type favoured by the NER in the era of the 10-hour day.

The signalman at Bolton Percy had arranged to turn the North Eastern train off the up Leeds line, on which it was running, on to the up Normanton line to follow the L&Y express as far as Church Fenton. This was because there was an empty mineral train bound for Gascoigne Wood Yard on the Leeds line at Ulleskelf. As the two passenger trains were running almost side by side it was necessary to check and hold the North Eastern train at Bolton Percy until the L&Y train cleared Ulleskelf, but the driver of the North Eastern engine ran past the signals and collided at about 40 mph with the brake van of the 60-wagon empty mineral train, which was stationery at Ulleskelf. Fortunately for the guard of that train, he was not in his van as he had gone to the box to remind the signalman of the presence of his train.

The badly damaged North Eastern engine was photographed at York on its way to Darlington a few days after the collision, which took place on 24th November 1906. No.85 was repaired, put back into traffic and continued to run until 1932.

TROUBLE WITH TRACK

After a sharp frost on the night of 25th/26th March 1907 the day developed into a fine spring morning and by mid-day it was hot and sunny, with hardly any breeze. By 1.45 pm, the rails in the cutting on the east side of Felling had buckled due to the heat of the sun. This fact was noticed by a dumb man crossing a bridge over the line and he pointed it out to the driver of a steam roller working nearby, who later said that the lines were like 'an elongated letter S'.

On realising the danger the steam roller driver ran along the top of the cutting to warn the signalman in Heworth box, advising him that he should put his signals to danger and stop the approaching train. This the signalman refused to do, asking 'Who are you and what has twisted the rails?', to which the driver replied 'Well, I can't say, but if you don't stop the train it will be a bad job'.

And a bad job it was when the 10.52 am Leeds-Newcastle (8.35 am from Liverpool) arrived on the scene. The engine and most of the train were derailed, some coaches falling over and coming to rest leaning on the cutting side. Seven London & North Western vehicles were damaged and eight passengers were seriously injured, of which two subsequently died. The engine was NER Class R 4-4-0 No.725.

OFF THE ROAD

As the LNWR 9.20 am train from Huddersfield to Stockport was running through Friezeland on 19th August 1909, it was partially derailed at the south-west end of the station. Fortunately it crossed a viaduct safely but when it reached the Stalybridge side the whole train was derailed. The engine, 0-6-2T No.1608 from Huddersfield shed, travelling chimney first, then dug into the formation and was completely turned round by its train, so that it came to rest facing the opposite way from which it had been running. Both driver and fireman were killed.

Photo: Collection the late Arthur Trevena

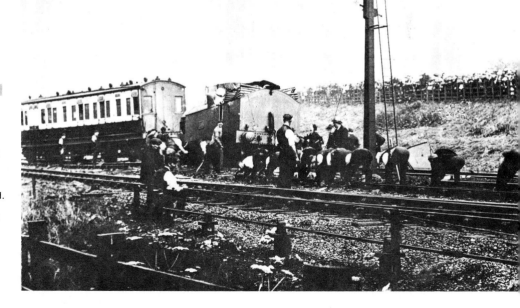

EXPRESS GOODS IN COLLISION

The unexplained derailments at Grantham, Salisbury and Shrewsbury have always aroused interest and speculation, but lesser known is the rear end collision which occurred at Darlington at about 12.50 am on 15th November 1910 when an up express goods ran past signals and collided with the rear of another goods standing on the main line outside Darlington station. The engine involved was NER Class S1 4-6-0 No.2115, one of the five engines built for working East Coast expresses but superseded by Atlantics.

The stationary goods was the 11.01 pm from Park Lane (Gateshead) to Hull and at the time the collision occurred the engine was away from its train putting some wagons into a siding. The second goods train was the 10.45 pm Newcastle-Leeds with a Tweedmouth crew. The driver ran past all his signals approaching Darlington and it was suggested at the enquiry that he was drowsy, or perhaps asleep, just prior to the collision and had been awakened by the explosion of a detonator at the North box as there were signs that the wheels had been skidding immediately prior to the collision. Suggestions were also made that the driver was a man of intemperate habits, but there was no proof that he had been drinking on the night prior to the collision.

The recovery of No. 2115.

DISASTER IN THE FELLS

The bridge over the Settle & Carlisle line of the Midland Railway at Ais Gill has latterly been used as a viewpoint for numerous photographs of preserved steam locomotives at work, but how many of the photographers know that within a few yards of the bridge 14 passengers perished on 2nd September 1913 when the 1.49 am from Carlisle crashed into the rear of the 1.35 am from Carlisle as the engine of the latter stood short of steam about half a mile north of Ais Gill box. The large number of passengers killed was due not only to the collision but also to the fire which followed, fuelled by gas escaping from the cylinders of the rear coaches of the leading train. The engine of the leading train was 4-4-0 No.993, and that of the second train was 4-4-0 No.446.

In this view the wreckage has been removed from the track.

Photo: BBC Hulton Picture Library

BRIDGE SWEPT AWAY

Torrential rain on the Grampians on 15th June flooded down the burns and caused a road bridge over the Baddengorm Burn to collapse. This resulted in the torrents backing up behind the debris of the bridge until the weight of water swept all aside and poured down the valley. As the torrent reached the bridge carrying the Highland Railway the 10.00 am Glasgow-Inverness ran on to it and the displaced track derailed the tender of the engine and the two leading coaches. Because of the derailment, the driver stopped his train with the two derailed coaches north of the bridge, the next three coaches on the bridge, and the rear coach south of the bridge. The driver just had time to walk back across the bridge to inform the guard of the derailment, when the bridge collapsed, dropping the fourth coach into the raging torrent. Five passengers were lost.

CROWBOROUGH 1916

PROBLEMS ON THE LBSCR

The use on passenger trains of engines with driving wheels leading has always aroused controversy. Certainly there have been derailments where this type of engine has been blamed, although often without conclusive evidence, but it does seem certain that when combined with other factors such as speed and the condition of the track, a derailment is more likely to occur than with an engine with a leading bogie. Such a derailment occurred on the morning of 3rd April 1916, when LBSCR 0-6-0T No.273, working the 8.00 am Tunbridge Wells to Brighton train, came to grief between Crowborough and Buxted.

Photo: Collection the late Arthur Trevena

See also page 2

ENGINES IN THE WARS

ABOVE: A derailment 'somewhere on the western front', although the board on the top lamp bracket reads *Depot d'Attache Dunkerque*. The engine is a ROD 2-8-0 of Great Central design and it appears as if the derailment was due to a sidelong collision as the engine is badly damaged on the side uppermost.

All photos: Courtesy the Trustees of the Imperial War Museum

RIGHT: This wartime derailment somewhere in France shows 60 cm gauge 2-6-2T No.1247, one of a hundred engines built by ALCO in 1917 for use behind the front.

BELOW: The exact location and date of this view are unknown but it was probably in France or Belgium in World War I. The engine is a Belgian 0-6-0 working for the Railway Operating Department. British 'Tommies' and troops from other countries are helping in the recovery operations. These engines were still at work in World War II.

A MILITARY RUNAWAY

On 15th September 1917 a set of ten NER 6-wheel coaches was being loaded with troops at Catterick Camp: no engine had been attached and any brakes that might have been applied were released. Consequently, as the coaches were standing on a falling gradient they moved off and gathered speed as they ran down the Camp Railway towards the North Eastern's Catterick Bridge station. However, before the coaches reached there they were derailed on a curve due to the excessive speed and three soldiers were killed or died from their injuries.

Three coaches were completely wrecked and the other seven were removed to York Carriage Works, where they arrived ten days after the accident. Six of these were immediately condemned but the sole survivor lasted until LNER days.

Four coaches in the set were Brake Thirds and the guard who had worked the train the previous night stated that he had left the set with the handbrake screwed on in all four vans, two of which were amongst the coaches completely destroyed in the derailment.

DOUBLE COLLISION IN TUNNEL

As the 2.10 am goods from Eastbourne started from a signal check at Earlswood just after 5.00 am on the morning of 18th April 1918 the train broke in two, the rear portion of three wagons and a van following the engine (2-6-0 No.340) and the front 56 wagons for some distance before coming to a stand in Redhill Tunnel. The guard took no action for some ten minutes and shortly after he finally left his van it was run into by 0-6-0 No.541 on the 11.40 pm goods from Portsmouth, which had entered the tunnel under clear signals. This was because the signalman at Quarry box, north of the tunnel, had given 'Train out of Section' for the front half of the train without noticing that it had no tail lamp.

Under the impression that nothing was amiss he also allowed the 4.00 am down special goods from Lillie Bridge to enter the tunnel and this train ran into the wreckage caused by the first collision, derailing the engine (0-6-0 No.536) and most of its train. For 40 ft the tunnel was filled with broken wagons and their contents and it took the best part of two days to clear the wreckage and remove the two derailed engines.

A CAMBRIAN DISASTER

The misunderstandings that led to the disastrous head-on collision at Abermule on 26th January have been told before, how confusion amongst the staff at that station resulted in a driver being given the wrong tablet, and how the two 4-4-0s on the express and slow trains met buffer to buffer at a closing speed estimated at 50 mph. This resulted in the boiler of engine No.95 being dislodged from the frames and turned round so that the firebox was to the front of the tender and the smokebox to the rear of the tender, with the engine frame reared up in the air.

The length of the two trains before the collision was about 250 yds, but after the collision the wreckage occupied some 180 yds, with the two engines and five coaches forming a tangled mass of wreckage in the centre.

Although most of the coaches had gas lighting no fire followed the collision.

TROUBLE AT YORK

The North Eastern Railway and the North Eastern Area of the LNER had a spate of accidents in the 1920s, including a number in the York area.

TOP RIGHT: On 14th February 1920 Class S2 4-6-0 No.787 collided head-on with No.788 of the same class at Skelton Bridge when both were working freight trains. No.788 was the only North Eastern engine fitted with a Weir feed-water-heater, with the pump and reservoir on the left-hand side.

RIGHT: A few weeks later, on 31st March, the unique three-cylinder compound 4-4-0 No.1619 was derailed whilst entering Platform 8 at York (now Platform 13).

BELOW: The North Eastern suffered a number of fires at engine sheds, usually with some engines inside. In 1921 one of the old roundhouses at the south end of York station was used for repairing wagon sheets but, to keep it out of the dirt associated with steam sheds, petrol-engined Officers' Inspection saloon No.3768 was housed in the building. On 22nd October 1921 the building was discovered to be on fire and the saloon was destroyed except for the frame and wheels. In 1923 a replacement car was built and allocated the same number. The pictures show the remains of the shed, with the remaining frames and wheels of the Inspection Saloon, and the Petrol Inspection Saloon before it was destroyed by fire. A similar car continued to run in the Newcastle area until 1939.

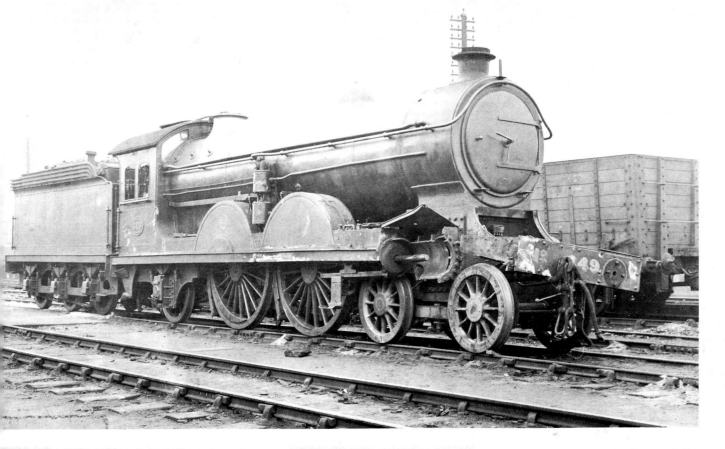

DRIVER MISSED THE SIGNALS

On Christmas Eve 1923 NER Class V Atlantic No.649 was working an East Coast express when the driver passed signals at danger at Belford and collided with Class 59 0-6-0 No.455. The right-hand cylinder of No.649 was broken off and some damage caused to the front of the engine, but the 0-6-0 came off much worse and lost its running plate and cab, and the tender lost its centre axle and wheels. The driver was suspended without pay for two weeks, taken off main line working, and reduced to a pilot (shunting) driver.

TOP: Class V 4-4-2 No.649 with broken right-hand cylinder and damaged buffer-beam.

LEFT: Class 59 0-6-0 No.455 seen at Gateshead for repair, minus running plate and cab and with tender wheels loaded into the coal space. The engine was repaired and put back into traffic until withdrawal in March 1927.

DRIVER FELL FROM TRAIN

After a nightime collision between an electric train and a goods train at Manors (Newcastle) on 7th August 1926 the body of the electric train driver was found — after three hours searching — near Heaton, about a mile back along the line. It was surmised that for some reason he was leaning out of the side door of the luggage compartment behind the driving cab, in an attempt to look into the leading passenger saloon, when he came into contact with the piers of an overbridge and fell out of the train.

After the collision, it was discovered that the spring-loaded safety button on the controller handle of the electric train was held securely depressed by tying it down with two handkerchiefs. This eventually led to a search of the line over which the train had travelled and the driver's body was found.

EXPRESS RAMS LIGHT ENGINE

On 27th February 1927, during light engine movements at Penistone, a signalman mistakenly allowed an LMS engine, 2-4-2T No.10760, on to the up main line when he accepted the 5.35 pm Manchester (Central) to London (Marylebone) express headed by LNER D10 4-4-0 No.5437 *Prince George*. The tank engine had arrived from Bradford and had gone to the turntable to turn ready for its return working to Huddersfield and it was as it was going back to its train at the down branch platform that the confusion arose. When the signalman cleared his signals for the express the driver of 10760 took them as referring to him and he started to move towards Sheffield to pass over the points which, after reversing, would take him on to the up branch to regain his train. The fireman noted the approaching express and warned his driver before jumping off the engine : the driver opened the regulator wide to lessen the severity of the collision and appears to have remained on the engine.

ANOTHER EXCURSION IN TROUBLE

Another disastrous head-on collision occurred at the south end of Darlington station on 27th June 1928, when C7 4-4-2 No.2164, at the head of an excursion returning from Scarborough, and running under clear signals, met B16 4-6-0 No.2369 as it was shunting some vans off its up parcels train. The B16 was pushed back 62 yards by the engine of the passenger train, which then fell on to its left-hand side. Severe telescoping occurred to some of the coaches and 25 passengers were killed and 45 severely injured.

DONCASTER 1929

RAILCAR CUT IN TWO

As an economy measure some of the Sunday services between Doncaster and Hull were provided by Sentinel steam railcar 220 *Waterwitch* running from Doncaster to Staddlethorpe to give connections with Leeds-Hull trains. As Doncaster shed had no Sentinel railcars the turn was worked by a Selby car and crew. On this fateful Sunday, 9th June, the driver of the car was probably misled by successive signals at clear because of closed boxes, and he over-ran the Marshgate Junction home signal and came to a stand on the junction, which D11 4-4-0 No.5511 *Marne* was approaching with a Leeds-London excursion.

In the ensuing sidelong collision the railcar was severely damaged, with the engine and boiler section detached from the passenger saloon and knocked down a low embankment. The railcar was not repaired!

LONGBRIDGE JUNCTION

HIDDEN FROM VIEW

W. Leslie Good was a noted photographer in the 1920s and 1930s and these views of derailed 0-6-4T No.2015 are from his collection. Where a derailed engine was not causing too much inconvenience it was the practice to leave it until the week-end and carry out the rerailing operations on a Sunday, when traffic was light. To hide the engine from the gaze of nervous passengers it was often completely covered with tarpaulins, as has happened in this case.

Photos: W.L. Good

GREAT BRIDGEFORD 1932

MYSTERIOUS DERAILMENT

This derailment occurred on 17th June 1932 as the 7.23 pm Crewe to Birmingham, with 4-4-0 No.5278 *Precursor*, was crossing from the up slow to the up fast line at the south end of Great Bridgeford station. The reason for the derailment was never satisfactorily resolved as it could not be proved whether it was due to the driver passing signals at danger, or the signalman resetting the crossover at the last minute. The engine was derailed and ploughed into soft earth at the side of the line, with the body of the first coach destroyed and with bogies torn off the underframe; the second coach ploughed through the first and was also badly damaged. Here again the engine was covered over until it could be removed.

Photo: BBC Hulton Picture Library

RAYNES PARK 1933

PERMANENT WAY PROBLEMS

As the 3.10 pm from Waterloo to Alton, headed by 0-4-4T No.107, was approaching Raynes Park on 25th May the engine and all five coaches of the train were derailed. Approaching on the up through line was 2-6-0 No.1621 on the 12.11 pm Southampton to Waterloo, and this hit the portions of the derailed coaches which were in its path, killing five passengers and injuring 34 on the Alton train, and seriously injuring the driver of No.1621. At the time of the derailment a permanent way gang was employed on lifting and packing the track and it was in no condition for a train to run over it at normal speed; no warning was given to the driver of No.107 on the down train, and the driver of the up express saw the coaches derailed in front of him when only some 30 yds away.

This view shows the damaged coaches of the Alton train.

Photo: BBC Hulton Picture Library

WINWICK 1934

SIGNALMAN FORGOT TRAIN

While a local train was held by signals at Winwick Junction on 28th September 1934 the signalman forgot that it was there and accepted a Euston to Blackpool express headed by 4-6-0 No.25648 *Queen of the Belgians*. This crashed into the back of the stationary train killing eleven passengers and staff. Although the crew of the local train carried out Rule 55 the fireman was just arriving at the box to remind the signalman of their presence when the collision occurred. No.25648 was damaged at the front end and was photographed at Crewe South shed nine days after the accident.

Photo: L.W. Perkins

BAD NIGHT AT WELWYN

Another example of a signalman forgetting a train occurred at Welwyn Garden City on 15th June 1935, a busy night when down expresses were running closely behind one another. The 10.48 pm for Newcastle, via the Coast, with C1 4-4-2 No.4411, was brought to a stand at Welwyn Garden City and when the signalman pulled off for the following train, headed by K3 2-6-0 No.4009, the forgotten No.4411 began to move. It was run into by the 10.53 pm Kings Cross to Leeds, killing 14 passengers and staff and seriously injuring 29 passengers.

LEFT: The damaged engine, K3 No.4009, awaiting repairs at Doncaster Works two weeks after the collision.

BELOW: The bodies of the rear coaches of the Newcastle train were destroyed and the frames compressed into a tangled mass of steel. This is the underframe of one coach being removed by the Peterborough steam crane. *Photo: John Adams*

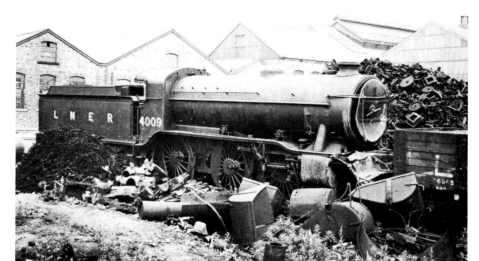

DEAD END

On this Sunday night, 28th June 1937, the 8.17 pm from Margate to London (Victoria) was running some 30 minutes late but it was intended to stop it specially at Swanley Junction to pick up some passengers who had missed their connection. The driver was not warned of this out-of-course stop, and confusion over the position of the distant signals led to the train running through the station at speed and the driver passing the home signal at danger. The points ahead were set for a dead-end siding ready for other movements to take place.

With a train not booked to stop the points should have been set for the main line to prevent an accident such as this, but the train ran into the siding and hit a wagon and two coaches standing there. These three vehicles were badly damaged and the coach nearest the buffer-stop was pushed into an electricity switching station compound, where it damaged and displaced the concrete pillars supporting the equipment.

Various coaches in the seven-coach train were telescoped and four passengers were killed. The engine was 4-4-0 No.1768.

Photos:
RIGHT: BBC Hulton Picture Library
OPPOSITE, TOP: H.C. Casserley
OPPOSITE, BOTTOM: BBC Hulton Picture
Library

BOMB DAMAGE OR WASHOUT?

This was a wartime casualty which happened on 13th September 1941. It has been suggested that the Q5 0-8-0 ran into a crater left by a German bomb dropped on the line from Durham to Consett, but no details have been discovered. However, Bridge Plate No.31, on the left, indicates a culvert or small bridge and a washout MAY have caused the accident.

POINTS HALF OPEN

The signalbox at Pannal Junction was abolished as an economy measure and replaced by electric points worked from Pannal station box. On this July 1944 day the 12.57 pm Leeds-Harrogate was derailed because of a points failure which left the points standing half open and set for neither the Crimple Junction nor Starbeck route. The engine, 4-4-2 No.720 came to rest on its right-hand side, with its train spreadeagled behind it.

TRAIN DIVIDED ON MAIN LINE

At about 5.40 am on the morning of 5th January 1946 a collision occurred at Browney signalbox, south of Durham on the East Coast main line, when the 11.15 pm Kings Cross-Newcastle headed by V2 2-6-2 No.4895 collided with B16 4-6-0 No.842 and the wreckage of some wagons behind it. It transpired that the up goods train headed by the B16 broke in two as it was accelerating from a signal check near Bridge House signalbox. The signalman at Bridge House noticed the gap between the two halves of the train as it passed his box and gave the 'train divided' bell signal to Browney box, where the engine and the leading wagons were stopped. Unfortunately all this had taken place on a falling gradient and the rear wagons and the van crashed into the wagons still attached to the engine, piling up wagons and derailing the engine.

Although the signalman had not cleared his signals for the down express the wreckage from the collision was resting on some of the signal wires and cleared the signals, so that the V2 hit the wreckage and was derailed: its train ploughed into a field on the down side, wrecking the 2nd, 3rd, 4th and 5th coaches. Ten passengers were killed.

As a result of the recommendations by the Inspecting Officer signalbox diagrams were modified to show the gradients on each side of the box: in this case the signalman had been under the mistaken impression that there was a stretch of rising gradient in the up direction north of his box which would halt the rear half of the goods train.

MULTIPLE CRASH AT POTTERS BAR

This multiple collision, which occurred on 10th February 1946, was caused by the signalman at Potters Bar moving the points under the first coach of an up local train from Hatfield, headed by N2 0-6-2T No.2679.

The engine ran into the buffer-stops at the end of the up slow line but the coaches were derailed and diverted on to the up main line, coming to a stand foul of the down main, on which the 9.45 pm Kings Cross to Edinburgh was approaching under clear signals (held off by the wreckage of the local train). The 9.45 pm train, headed by V2 2-6-2 No.4876, collided with the derailed coaches and almost immediately the 5.00 pm Bradford to Kings Cross train ran into

the combined wreckage: this train was headed by another V2, No.4833, which fell over on to its left-hand side.

Only two passengers in the Hatfield train were killed: although over 1000 passengers were carried aboard the two expresses.

ABOVE: Rerailing V2 No.4876 at Potters Bar: this engine was working the 9.45 pm from Kings Cross.

ABOVE: The engine of the Bradford-Kings Cross train, V2 No.4833, on its side. The engine of the down train, No.4876, can be seen in the background.

ABOVE: One of the damaged coaches of the Hatfield train.

DONCASTER 1947

A MASS OF WRECKAGE

On a very busy August Saturday, 9th August 1947, the 1.25 pm Kings Cross to Leeds ran into the rear of the 1.10 pm Kings Cross to Leeds at Doncaster. The first train, headed by A3 4-6-2 No.50 *Persimmon* was moving off after a signal stop when the following train, headed by V2 2-6-2 No.936, ran into the back of it at about 40 mph. Each train carried some 700 passengers. The force of the collision was largely absorbed by the rear three coaches of the first train and their underframes were rolled into a tangled mass of wreckage as the V2 ploughed into them. Most of the casualties — 21 passengers killed and 188 injured — were in the leading train.

The collision was again due to a signalman forgetting the leading train and clearing his signals for the second.

TROUBLE ON THE SOUTHERN

Another rear-end collision took place three months later, on 26th November 1947, when SR 4-6-0 No.453 *King Arthur* ran into a train headed by Lord Nelson 4-6-0 No.860 *Lord Hawke* west of Farnborough. The trains involved were the 3.05 pm Bournemouth to Waterloo and the 12.15 pm Ilfracombe to Waterloo. The first train was standing at an automatic signal put at danger by a power failure. Again the three rear coaches of the leading train suffered severely, but only two passengers were killed. A third train, the 4.00 pm Salisbury-Waterloo, travelling on the up local line was stopped clear of the wreckage.

It transpired that the signalman at Fleet had given misleading information to the drivers of the Ilfracombe and Salisbury trains and had not ensured that both lines were clear after the signalling power supply failure.

NEW SOUTHGATE 1948

DRAMA ON THE TOP LINK

The well-known Kings Cross driver Bill Hoole was involved in this derailment on 17th July 1948, when working the 7.50 pm Edinburgh-Kings Cross with A2 4-6-2 No.60508 *Duke of Rothesay*. The bogie of the engine was derailed by poorly maintained track in Barnet tunnel and when the bogie struck a crossing south of the tunnel it destroyed the track and the whole train was derailed. The engine fell on to its right-hand side and slid on the rails of the up main line for about 100 yds, passing under a three-arch road bridge without damaging the piers.

Driver Hoole stepped off the engine only slightly injured when it came to rest, but the fireman jumped from the derailed engine and was struck by the coaches and killed. Subsequent measurements pointed to faulty track being the cause of the derailment, although Driver Hoole was exceeding the 60 mph limit by about 10 mph.

ELECTRICAL FAULT WRECKS TRAIN

The 2.21 pm Liverpool Street to Ipswich was approaching Bethnal Green station when a pair of facing points leading from the down main to the down suburban line operated as the train was passing over them. At the time two linesmen were trying to trace a fault in the relay room at the signalbox and, although not conclusively proved, it was thought that the wire guard on a test lamp being used by one of the linesmen must have touched two terminals, providing a false feed of current which operated the facing points as the train was passing over them.

The engine, B1 No.61046, remained on the down main line but the leading coach was dragged along broadside until it mounted the station platform and struck an overhead gantry. Fortunately the four passengers in the leading coach escaped unhurt on this 4th day of September 1953.

Photo: BBC Hulton Picture Library

BROKEN BOGIE

On 1st September 1955 I was making a round trip York-London-Bristol-York, so that when an acquaintance rang my wife from Peterborough and told her there had been a railway accident that day she got quite a shock! The one-off W1 4-6-4 No.60700 (rebuilt from the Gresley water tube boilered engine 10000) was derailed at Westwood Junction when the faulty leading bogie struck facing points. Due to a flaw the right-hand bogie frame plate had broken as the engine pulled away from Peterborough, but the derailment was immediately noticed by the driver, who rapidly brought the train to a standstill from the 20 mph it had attained after the Peterborough stop.

The engine was derailed to the left, towards the former LMS line, and it was actually rerailed — minus bogie — on the LMS tracks; hence the use of a Midland 4F 0-6-0 to remove the engine, which was repaired and put back into traffic.

DISASTER IN THE FOG

On this foggy December evening the driver of the 4.56 pm Cannon Street to Folkestone and Ramsgate train passed signals at danger and collided with the rear of the 10-coach electric train forming the 5.18 pm from Charing Cross to Hayes.

The eighth coach of the electric train was destroyed and the engine of the second train (4-6-2 No.34066 *Spitfire*) was derailed and struck a column of a large girder overbridge carrying the Nunhead to Lewisham flyover. This allowed part of the bridge to collapse, with the girders crushing the leading three coaches of the Ramsgate train.

Altogether 89 passengers lost their lives — 37 in the electric train (which was carrying some 1,500 passengers) and 49 in the steam train (with approximately 700 passengers).

The driver of the steam train was tried twice on a charge of manslaughter; on the first occasion the jury could not agree, and at the second trial he was acquitted.

The accident occurred on 6th December 1957 and this view shows the clearing-up operations, taken from the bridge which collapsed on to the train below.

Photo: Keystone

A3 ON THE PLATFORM

A most spectacular accident occurred at York on Monday 5th August 1958, involving A3 4-6-2 No.60036 *Colombo*. Because it was a Bank Holiday the working had been altered and the driver was under the impression that he was running into a through platform (No.9) when, in fact, he was running into a bay platform (No.12). The engine hit the buffers at speed, tearing off the bogie, and the front end rode up on the bogie wheels, ending with the smokebox in the air and the front buffer-beam just touching the footbridge. When the engine came to rest the centre pair of driving wheels marked the original position of the buffer-stop. In the afternoon of the same day *Colombo* was drawn back on to the track and removed to the shed by an 8F 2-8-0, to await repairs at Doncaster Works.

PROBLEMS ON
THE NCB

For many years the Lambton, Hetton & Joicey group of collieries in County Durham worked trainloads of coal to the Lambton Staiths at Sunderland over the railway company's lines using their own engines. This practice continued under National Coal Board and British Railways ownership and this view illustrates a sidelong collision between NCB No.31 and BR J27 0-6-0 No.65892 on 8th June 1960.

A MOMENT OF ABERRATION

Single line operation between Laindon and Pitsea meant that on 18th April 1961 the 12.25 pm Fenchurch Street to Shoebury- ness had to run over the up line in the down direction as work proceeded on electrification.

Because of the 1 in 110 gradient, trap points were installed in the up line and an 'experienced and properly equipped man' was appointed to clip the points in the closed position for down trains, to which the points became facing. Unfortunately 'in a moment of aberration' this man clipped the points in the open position, thus derailing the train, to which he had given a 'clear' handsignal. The engine, BR Class 4 2-6-4T No.80075, was derailed to the right, and the two leading coaches were telescoped by the weight of those following.

A DELTIC IN TROUBLE

In thick fog, on 15th December 1961, an empty coaching stock train headed by Deltic No.D9012 ran into the rear of an up braked goods whilst travelling on the up goods line under Permissive Block Working. In the collision the brake van of the goods was thrown on to the up main line, and it also fouled the down main line. Three or four minutes later another braked goods on the down main line, headed by A3 4-6-2 No.60078 *Night Hawk*, hit the van at about 50 mph and turned over on to its left-hand side, followed in another three to four minutes by a third braked goods, headed by V2 2-6-2 No.60977, hitting the wreckage whilst travelling at 35 mph on the up main line! The result was a huge pile of wrecked wagons and three damaged engines, although the main lines were opened again within 42 hours.

Photos: P. N. Townend

EDINBURGH WAVERLEY 1966

PROBLEMS FOR DP2

In August 1966 the experimental diesel locomotive DP2 was derailed at Edinburgh Waverley station. DP2 was recovered undamaged, but it was not long before it was in more serious trouble.

THIRSK 1967

MORE PROBLEMS FOR DP2

Whilst working the 12 noon Kings Cross to Edinburgh express on 31st July 1967 the driver of DP2 saw a cloud of dust swell up some distance ahead of him. He suspected something was wrong and braked, but before his train stopped the engine hit some derailed cement wagons off a train travelling on the down slow. DP2 was severely damaged and the wagons were also struck by the coaches in the train. Unfortunately, seven passengers were killed and 45 injured. *Photo: John M. Boyes*

BACK ON THE RIGHT LINES

An essential part of the recovery equipment required after serious accidents is the steam crane, although diesel-powered cranes are now finding increasing favour on British Rail. This fine view, taken on 13th July 1969, shows two BR cranes rerailing Hymek No.D7048.

Photo: T.W. Nicholls

WORCESTER 1976

END OF A 'WESTERN'

On the evening of Friday 2nd January 1976 high winds brought down trees and telegraph poles between Droitwich Spa and Worcester Tunnel Junction signalbox, severing communication. Consequently Time Interval Working was introduced and operated satisfactorily throughout the night. The following morning, a light engine (Class 52 No.1055) was admitted into the section ten minutes after a one-van parcels train (No.31.241 and a GUV).

Due to delays on the outward journey the driver of No.52.1055 had refused to work his booked return train from Bescot to Gloucester and insisted on returning light engine. In so doing, his locomotive collided at speed with the preceding parcels train, the driver of which had stopped to report his position to the signalman at Worcester Tunnel Junction box. The driver of No.52.1055 and the guard riding in the leading cab were both killed, and their engine was withdrawn two days later.

Photo: T.W. Nicholls